One Hundred Poems of CHOKHA MELA

Translated & Introduced by

CHANDRAKANT KALURAM MHATRE

Sitaram Mhatre Foundation
Navi Mumbai
www.sitarammhatre.foundation

One Hundred Poems of Chokha Mela

Translated & Introduced by
Chandrakant Kaluram Mhatre

Published by
SITARAM MHATRE FOUNDATION
Registered Office
Sitaram Smaran, 896, Sector 19B,
Koparkhairane, Navi Mumbai 400709
Email: info@sitarammhatre.foundation

Second Edition: January 2024

ISBN (Paperback): 978-81-960911-2-5

Cover Photograph
Chandrakant Kaluram Mhatre

Proofreading, Typesetting, Cover & Book Design
Mhatre's Translation & Allied Services
Navi Mumbai, MS, India

To
my grandfather,
Late Sitaram G. Mhatre,
for him forgiveness came so naturally,
even when it was not
the least deserved
by its recipient

CONTENTS

FOREWORD

It's been almost nine years, since I first published *One Hundred Poems of Chokha Mela* to commemorate the centenary year of Guru Rabindranath Tagore's *One Hundred Poems of Kabir* (1915), as Rabindranath's book holds a special place in the history of Indian literature, being perhaps the very first attempt by an Indian to translate a Bhakti poet into English. Having published it as a commemorative project back-to-back after *One Hundred Poems of Tukaram* in the same year viz. 2015, I was painfully aware of the typos in my translation of and introduction to Sant Chokha Mela's poems, but I could not begin work on its revised edition sooner, since my third book in that series, *The Autobiography of Sant Bahinabai* (2023) proved to be a daunting challenge and kept me busy for next seven years. In a happy turn of events, completion of Bahinabai's translation coincided with *One Hundred Poems of Chokha Mela* becoming a prescribed text for "Indian Literature in Translation" course of M.A. (Honours) in English & M.A. (Honours with Research) in English programmes of the University of Mumbai and I could devote time to this second edition (along with its bilingual edition) in which I have tried to get rid of the imperfections that could possibly hamper proper understanding and appreciation of Chokhoba's poems.

Repeating myself, I again take this opportunity to congratulate the University of Mumbai's Dept. of English & its HOD, Dr. Rajesh Karankal for daring to be so inclusive as to become perhaps the very first Dept. of English in India to include Sant Chokha Mela in its curriculum. May Chokhoba's poems about his lived experiences of discrimination be our guiding light in these divisive times that we live in.

Navi Mumbai
January 2024

Chandrakant Kaluram Mhatre

INTRODUCTION

History of discrimination among human beings on one basis or other is as old as the history of humankind itself. In fact, one dares to state that the discrimination in one form or other has been the foundation of human civilization in all places and in all times. What is assuring in this deeply murky history is the equally resonating fact that the history of rebellions against all kinds of discrimination is as old as the origin of discrimination itself. At some points in history, these rebellions have been limited to individuals; at other times, entire societies have stood up in rebellion against the oppressions of discrimination. Some of these rebellions were brutally crushed using monstrous force, while a good number of rebellions have been so successful that discriminating powers were wiped out of the face of the earth. One such rebellion took place in Maharashtra in the thirteenth century and went on for centuries to come. It was one of the most successful rebellions ever and that too without using violence at all - even verbal violence was unthinkable to these rebels! They did not believe in doing away with the practitioners of discrimination - instead, they successfully attempted to do away with the mentality that establishes and encourages discrimination in the name of caste /class /creed /colour /gender. They were all followers of Varkari Sampraday, a unique sect within Hinduism founded by Sant Dnayndev and Sant Namdev in the last decade of the thirteenth century. So successful was this rebellion of the Varkaris against discrimination that the most impactful voice against such oppression came from a person belonging to one of the most downtrodden communities of that time: Chokha Mela!

He was born in the Mahar community which lay at the bottom of the caste hierarchy prevalent in the contemporary society. Of course, he was not to have any education even in the remotest sense of the word. Yet, such was the influence of the two founding fathers and other saints of the Varkari Sect that Chokha Mela could compose poetry of the highest order. Poetry that has stood the test of time for last seven hundred years and has become the finest example of the expression of human angst caused by the oppressive societal norms. Each poem by Chokha Mela, or Chokhoba as he was fondly called by his peers, stands testimony to the inhuman treatment that was meted out to large sections of society in the name of religion. Each of his poems is a cry of the bereaved soul that has been deprived of its humanness itself. Each of the poem is a powerful statement against the repression that a handful carried out against the masses. Such is the intensity of these poems that their reader feels the very angst that the Poet must have undergone. Such is the grip that these poems take over the reader's mind that one feels their guts being wrenched, remembering the agony of the Poet's expressions long after the poems have been read and the book kept aside.

What gives Chokhoba's poems such a power over their readers? In their very basic form, they are 'poems of protest' and one has to accept that any protest literature has the limitations of contemporaneity. Yesterday's intense protest poem may appear entirely lifeless today. Yesteryear's immensely moving protest poem may come across as mundane altogether today. But this certainly is not the case with Chokhoba's poems which were mostly composed in the first decades of the fourteenth century, making them exactly seven hundred years old. These centuries, however, have not succeeded in diminishing the power of the poems even by a degree. In fact, given our times' essential belief in the human rights of every individual, these poems gain much more power to move than they had earlier. How has Chokhoba succeeded in overcoming the basic limitation of protest literature then? Answers to this fundamental question will vary from reader to reader, but for me what matters the most is the fact that Chokha Mela did not use his poems as a means of protest but self-expression. And it is this genuine expression of his anguished heart that has given his poems the timelessness that they have been enjoying from the times even before the birth of Geoffrey Chaucer.

What kind of self-expression does one come across in Chokha Mela's poems? The entire spectrum of human feelings, doubts, epiphanies, predicaments and realizations of the highest order are the stuff that these poems are made of. What is significant is that all these expressions in these poems are easily the experiences of the common-most human being, the Poet's sainthood does not raise its spectre between him and his reader. On every word of these poems, the reader gets the feeling that what is being expressed is exactly their own heart's cry - no matter at which place and in which times they are born! Chokhoba's expression becomes the expression of each of his reader, overcoming all the barriers of social, cultural, historical and geographical restrains. This is what has enabled his poems to resound in every age and every place. They have been communicating with their readers (erstwhile listeners, for his poems were mainly sung/recited) the essential human predicament - having to choose between one's lot and one's aspirations!

What was it that Chokha Mela aspired for? What was it with his aspirations that went against his predestined 'lot'? To understand this, we will have to traverse seven hundred years back to the thirteenth century. There are no convincing records about Chokha Mela's birth year or birth place, but we know for sure that he was a contemporary of Sant Dnyandev and Sant Namdev. He has even described the occasion of Dnyandev's 'Samadhi Eternal'[1] in one of his poems, accurately recording the date of that momentous event in the history of Varkari Sect. Also, his poems elaborating upon his discipleship of Sant Namdev give us a fair idea about his times. However, the best source to determine Chokhoba's times is the biographical poems of Namdev himself who has recorded important events in the lives of all his contemporary saints with historical accuracy. All these literary evidences squarely place Chokhoba in the final decades of the thirteenth century and the initial decades of the fourteenth century. His place of birth though remains a bone of contention. What we know for sure is that he spent a considerable part of his life in Pandharpur2 - of course far away from the main settlement owing to his caste.

Chokha Mela was born in the Mahar community which was considered to be the 'untouchables' by the then so-called higher castes owing to the menial work that was assigned to them. The Mahars were to maintain the cleanliness and the hygiene in the society mainly by disposing off the carcasses of dead animals including the cattle. And it was this society-assigned work of theirs on the basis of which the same society considered them as source of pollution and avoided even their shadows, let alone their touch. They were denied every single human right that we uphold so religiously today. There was no education for them, no possibility of changing their profession and no any other means of livelihood like land. Basically, they were dispossessed of their human status itself and had to survive begging for the leftovers of the higher caste people for this was how they were paid for all their back-breaking scavenging work. Even when these stale leftovers were given to them, they were dropped into their bamboo baskets from such a distance to avoid the pollution that would cause by an accidental touch! In case of such a calamity of having polluted by the touch of such a person, the higher castes would immediately resort to ablution to wash off the effects of that pollution.

Such was the 'lot' of Chokha Mela. So, when he arrived in Pandharpur with his wife Soyara somewhere in the 1280-90 CE, he had no option but to erect a hut for themselves on the opposite bank of River Bhima on whose bank the main settlement and the Vitthal temple was situated. Chokha had reached Pandharpur2 having heard about the revolution that the Varkaris were trying to bring in the contemporary society by advocating complete annihilation of all kinds of discrimination. While all his brethren were happy with their lot, Chokha aspired for something better, something nobler than mere sense-perception existence that he has described in his poems as:

My own community
Have to eat impious
Liquor and meat
Their meals comprise

or

Sycophants, thieves, womanizers
Corrupt through and through
Debased existence for eternity
Is their destiny.

What sets Chokha apart from this 'debased existence' is his desire to rise above his lot. He desired for a better life - not in the material sense of that much-maligned phrase but something far superior than that. He did not desire for better food, better house or better clothing, instead he desired for the human dignity which was not to be associated with his caste at all. It was almost equal to asking for a moon! But that was what Chokha desired for - to be treated as an equal, which gets an expression in his poems thus:

To avoid my touch
No one seats near me
Chokha says such is
Life mine

or

No one accepts me
In their company
"Get lost from here"
Says one and all

and

Outcaste that we are
What rights we have?
Everyone shoos us
Far away.

Throughout his poems, Chokha keeps asking questions about his rights, or rather their absence. This awareness of one's rights is something that shapes much of his character. He is so assured of his own worth as a poet, as a devotee of the Lord Vitthal that his low caste status does not fill him with the kind of diffidence that plagues almost anyone who has been subjugated to such kind of extreme repression as the Mahar community. This psychological strength is the most valuable gift that Chokha received from his Varkari mentors. This strength is what enabled him to question all the injustices heaped upon him in the name of untouchability and pollution:

Then how can one be pure
And the other impure
If the origin of pollution
Is our bodies?

and

Pollution of the Five
Within one body
Then pure in the world
How can be any?

The very fact that a member of the lowest caste could question the hegemony of the predominant classes signifies a lot about the extent of the revolution that the Varkaris had set in motion. That such poems were not and could not be suppressed and destroyed speaks volume about the eminence that Chokha Mela had earned among these circles. One gets a distinct idea of Chokha's eminence when one comes across him questioning the sacrosanct scriptures itself in his poems:

Pollution for Vedas
Pollution for Shastras
Puranas are filled with
Demeaning pollution.

However, all was this hunky-dory only till Chokha was among his Varkari companions. The moment he would step out of that enlightened circle, he would have to face the atrocities at the hands of the higher echelons of the society, especially the Brahmins. How could a Mahar rise to the status of sainthood? How could someone, who is to be but trampled upon at every instance, be allowed to be revered by others socially superior to him. That was a challenge to the very existence of the caste hierarchy. Blinded by this rage and the pathetic belief in their own superiority, the Brahmins of Pandharpur began to persecute Chokha and his entire family every which way possible. This persecution was not only limited to verbal humiliation but went even beyond physical assaults: they accused Chokha of stealing from the Vitthal temple. One of the most well-known of Chokhoba's poems speaks of this incident:

Rush forth, O Vithu, do not walk so slow
The priests beat me up, whatever my crime

"How has Vithoba's garland reached your neck?"
They curse me, call me Mahar, "The Lord's been defiled"

Chokhoba's stay in Pandhari had become almost impossible but his love for his deity Vitthal and his Guru Namdev was so great that he could never think of leaving Pandhari and faced all these atrocities with immense courage. At times, such cruel was the treatment given to Chokhoba that his heart was filled with doubts regarding his own beliefs, even his faith. These excruciating moments have got such an expression in his poems that one feels the strongest tug possible at the heart while reading them - making one wonder how would have this man undergone with all these miseries and sorrows and yet retain his faith!

Chokhoba's faith is indeed unique. He loved the deity - even at the risk of his dear life - which he was not even able to see, for he was not ever allowed to enter the temple of Lord Vitthal. All he could reach was up to the door of the temple, waiting outside with folded hands to be allowed inside. This is the most poignant image in all of Chokha's poems:

Choked up Chokha
Stands at His door
Entreating the Lord
With folded hands.

It almost takes form of a powerful symbol when one reads his poems in a succession with this image hitting one constantly, appearing in so many different forms and dimensions:

Not speak any further
That alone would be wise
Will become a rock
Lying at Your door

or

Give me place
At Your door
This is all, O Lord
I ask of You

and

At His door Chokha Mela
Beholds Vitthal with own eyes.

In the end, however, the Brahmins succeeded in making Chokha leave Pandharpur as he was among the Mahars who were made to work on the construction of town-wall at a nearby place called Mangalavedha. In many decades, for the first time Chokha was separated from his beloved Lord and the poems that he composed during his stay there are distinctly poignant:

My end is nigh
It seems to me
What was destined
Has happened

From birth, dependent
Have been servant Yours
Now in the end
I lie far away.

When one reads these poems knowing the historical fact that Chokha could never return to Pandahrpur from Mangalvedha, they begin to signify on a different level altogether. During the construction of the town-wall, a portion of it collapsed, killing a number of Mahar labourers under it - Chokha being one of them. Namdev brought his bones back to Pandharpur and built his Samadhi (final resting place) right in front of the Vitthal temple's main entrance. Today, anyone who visits the Vitthal temple at Pandharpur, first pays their obeisance to Chokhoba and then only enters the temple to see the Lord. For others this Samadhi might stand for many other things, for me it stands as an emblem of the victory of the indomitable human aspirations over Fate.

I find Chokhoba's poems extremely tragic in tone and equally cathartic in function. No doubt they are very significant as social documents, recording the protest against caste discrimination. But fortunately, they transcend this utility and enter the realm of pure art that makes human life much more meaningful. It is high time that we stop looking at this poet as a mere social documenter and begin to appreciate and assess him as a poet-artist of the highest order.

Navi Mumbai — Chandrakant Kaluram Mhatre
May 2015

NOTES:

1 Yogis of highest order would bring their life to completion by absorbing themselves into the deepest possible meditation, attaining absolute unison with the Creation, while seated in a sealed underground chamber.

2 Pandharpur, also known as Pandhari, is a town in Solapur district of Maharashtra, that houses the temple of Lord Vitthal, also known as Pandurang, the Supreme deity of the Varkari Sect.

|| 1 ||

Sugarcane misshapen, but the sap is not
Why be charmed with mere appearance?

Bow misshapen, but the arrow is not
Why be charmed with mere appearance?

River misshapen, but the water is not
Why be charmed with mere appearance?

Chokha misshapen, but the faith is not
Why be charmed with mere appearance

|| 2 ||

I saw, I saw
The Lord of yogis
Rukmadevi's Spouse
From Pandhari

Owing to Pundalik[1]
For twenty-eight eons
Has assumed cherub-form
On the banks of Bhima

Cows and calves
Together with Vaishnavs
Dance the cowherds
For the love of Vitthal

Chokha Mela there
Bows to touch feet
Lies prostrate
At His door

1 The legend says that it was for Pundalik that Lord Krishna arrived in Pandhari and assumed the form of Lord Vitthal. Thus, Pundalik is accorded the honour of being the originator of the cult of Lord Vitthal.

|| 3 ||

Hearing of the ears
Smelling of the nose
Tasting of the tongue
Vitthal mine

Makes tongue speak
Makes eyes see
Makes organs perform
Vitthal mine

Makes breath move
Keeps mind restrained
Distinct from nothingness
Vitthal mine

Who bestows bliss on bliss
Epiphany on epiphany
Unadulterated Being in all
Vitthal mine

Origin of the Origin
Source of the Absolute
Chokha says the Gain Supreme
Vitthal mine

|| 4 ||

His visage splendid
Yellow sarong drape
Garland Vaijayanti[1]
Adorning neck

He, the Dusky[2], is
My nearest and dearest
Let my eyes see Him
O great Saints

Great many rescued
In so disparate manners
All the Scriptures glorify
His benevolence

Chokha says Vedas
And Shastras[3] who manifests
He alone protects us
Disparately

1 One of the fourteen jewels extracted through the Great Churning of the Sea
2 Vitthal, being an incarnation of Krishna, has the same dark complexion, hence addressed thus.
3 Schools of Indian philosophy also called Darshan

|| 5 ||

Unadulterated[1] good, unadulterated good
One and only Pandurang mine

Bliss is at His feet
Reserve of all good deeds

Enormous sins got absolved
Unadulterated goodness of His name

At His door Chokha Mela
Beholds Vitthal with own eyes

1 The Marathi word *chokhat* (चोखट) has familial ties with the Poet's name, Chokha (चोखा), leading to beautiful wordplay throughout the poem. It also bears great significance when one takes into consideration the fact that the community, in which the Poet was born, was considered to be impure by the so-called higher echelons of the society.

|| 6 ||

Let's clap with hands
Let's raise the flag
Let's walk down the path
Towards Pandhari

Town square of Pandhari
And its public places
All are thronged
By Varkaris

Flocks of flags
Converge countless
Loud acclamations
On the banks of Bhima

The Name of the Lord
Rids of fears and worries
So speaks Geeta
And Bhagvat

Come, o fallen, debauched
And get purified here
Proclaims with faith
Chokha Mela

||7||

Chants of Vitthal, Vitthal
Reverberates entire Pandhari

Rings the name of the Lord
Amidst the flocks of flags

Nivrutti, Dnyandev, Sopan[1]
And countless other Vaishnav

Praise of the Lord exuberant
Chokha prostrates on their feet

1 Dnyandev and his brothers, Nivrutti & Sopan, were Chokha Mela's contemporaries and were accompanied by him on their numerous excursions for the spread of the teachings of the Varkari Sect.

|| 8 ||

Wandered a lot
From lands to lands
But my mind settled
In none of them

Great many holy places
Have returned from
But like my mind
I am raging insane

Great many icons
Have seen, heard too
Mind has remained still
Unrestrained

Chokha says on seeing
Pandhari, the Heaven on earth
All agonies of mind
Have absconded

|| 9 ||

Unadulterated Chokha Mela
Celebrates the name of the Lord

Outcaste Mahar I am
Erstwhile borne as Neel[1]

Slandered the Lord then
Hence reborn as Mahar

Chokha says pollution
Is the fruit of our past deeds

1 One of the great warriors in Lord Rama's Army of the Apes from the Ramayana

|| 10 ||

We experienced bliss
We experienced bliss
We beheld the Lord
Within our body

The Observed vanished
The observer hid
The Lord's miracle
Within our body

The Lord behind and in front
Any place without Him?
In heart, we found the Lord
Within our body

Chokha says the Lord
I beheld in Pandhari
Standing on the brick
By the banks of Bhima

|| 11 ||

Karma gave up
Religion gave up
All disappeared
Then and there

Mores gave up
Taboos overcame
All disappeared
Then and there

Vedas gave up
Shastras gave up
All disappeared
Then and there

Chokha says mine
Doubt dissolved
Within my body
Found the Lord

|| 12 ||

Rush forth, O Vithu, do not walk so slow
The priests beat me up, whatever my crime

"How has Vithoba's garland reached your neck?"
They curse me, call me Mahar, "The Lord's been defiled"

The dog at Your door, do not disown me, O Benefactor
Pray, Almighty Lord, you are responsible for me

With folded hands, Chokha entreats the Lord
By these my words, pray, do not get offended

|| 13 ||

If this is what you intended
Why did you give me birth?

Abandoned me, giving birth
What has so hardened your heart?

Wherever gone in my time of need
To whose rescue have you rushed?

Chokha says, O Lord
Do not disown me, O Keshav

|| 14 ||

Father you are mine
Mother of the world
Why not show mercy
Any on us?

Why this household
Imposed on me
That separates us
From each other?

Birth, dotage, death
For us joys, sorrows
What pleasure watching
All this, O Lord?

Choked up Chokha
Stands at His door
Entreating the Lord
With folded hands

|| 15 ||

Outcaste I am called, O Lord
Not knowing how to serve You

We, the lowly, know only this
To sing Your praise aloud

I wish only for the leftovers
Of the Saints, a humble servant

Chokha says, O Lord
You've accepted wretched me

|| 16 ||

Lowly caste is mine, O Lord
How would I get to serve You?

They tell me to stay far away
How would I get to meet You?

At the slightest touch of my hand
They observe prompt ablution

O my Govinda, Gopala
Begs for mercy Chokha Mela

|| 17 ||

Without toiling hard
Got exhausted, O Lord
Don't see shelter for me
Anywhere

We are hounded
By our own Karma
Whomever shall we
Hold responsible?

Have got entrapped
In debts of foes
Don't know in quicksand
How got stuck

Chokha says, listen
Lord Resident of Pandhari
Who will rescue us
If not you?

|| 18 ||

Whom should we claim
To be ours, O Lord?
Pray, tell us who else
Would rush for us?

You are the Almighty
Of all the Three Worlds
The Lord of the lords
Thence this supplication

You had accepted me
Why forsake me now?
Think through and through
Of this, O my Parents

Dependent of yore
I am yours, O Lord
I beg for Your mercy
Earnestly says Chokha

|| 19 ||

Not seeking respect
Nor disrespect
Both have relevance
None for me

Joys or sorrows
Fruits of past deeds
Born of Karma
Erstwhile

Birth and death
Is our destiny
In vain to desire, despair
After these

Chokha says this
Be my resolution
To endure this verity
Henceforth

|| 20 ||

O Lord, why to put me
In this predicament?
Solve this riddle
For me, please

The Mighty should be
True to reputation
You ought to realise this
On Your own

Outcaste that we are
What rights do we have?
Everyone shoos us
Far away

Chokha says such
Demeaning existence
I am in a dilemma
What should I do?

|| 21 ||

Now for how long
Should I hold back, O Lord?

Have been guarding Your door
You seem to have disowned me

This is no good conduct
Suits Your stature well though

Chokha says what to say
Ruined myself on own accord

|| 22 ||

I am terror stricken
That now nothing will work

Now I am obstructed
By the mightier than the mighty

I seek my own good
I get only pain and anguish

On the path of happiness
I find nothing but sorrows

Whatever my endeavours
Chokha says are shattered

|| 23 ||

Privileged I am
To supplicate at your feet
You the Almighty
You know it well

Among all castes
Created mine the basest
"Pollution, Pollution"
Uttered each moment

No one accepts me
In their company
"Get lost from here"
Says one and all

Chokha says, O Lord
Please accept me
That alone can give
Joy to me

|| 24 ||

What makes You indulge
In discrimination, O Lord?
This is what puzzles me
To no end

One gets throne
One gets robes
One has to roam
But naked

One gets coarse food
One gets banquets
One gets no dried bread
Despite pleading

One gets great wealth
One gets kingdom
One goes begging
Lands to lands

It seems the only justice
At Your place is this
Chokha says, O Lord
Such is my Karma

|| 25 ||

Wherever I go
I am in bondage
In order to break free
I endeavour ever

But I fail to find
Any solution to it
Evermore I sink
In deeper waters

One after another
Fall strikes on me
Despite trying to evade
What should I do?

Chokha says here
All my efforts fail
Rush forth, my Mother
O Lord Vitthal

|| 26 ||

Why I alone
Have to consider this?
I do not understand
The reason at all

How to serve You?
And express devotion?
I fail to understand
Detachment any

Apart from this
I have no right
How should I
Go about it?

Chokha says this
I remember all the time
Extremely difficult
It looks ahead

|| 27 ||

Does mother need to be
Taught by the babe?
Of her own accord
Embraces it

The same it would be
At Your place
Thus believing
Walked all the way

But why it seems today
Gone entirely wrong?
It seems by the power
Of our past deeds

Chokha says I do not
Blame You at all
Our Karma seems to be
Overpowering

|| 28 ||

Patience my mind has
None, none at all, O Lord

Have been so tormented in life
Have turned into springs of sorrows

There may be joy in accepting Fate
But in end it is nothing but sorrow

Became carrier of burdens
By futile pursuits got pillaged

Have mercy, O Lord of Pandhari
Chokha surrenders on Your feet

||29||

Canine or swine, give me birth as feline
But in the home of Vaishnavs alone

That only can make my heart content
I would not beg then for anything else

Blessed leftovers I will savour ardently
Will keep lying around admiringly

Chokha says anyone going to Pandhari
I will lie prostrate happily at their feet

|| 30 ||

How far should I
Keep worrying over?
Why do you, O Lord
Know this not?

Trapped inside the net
Caught by the hook
I suffer infinitely
But in vain

Lust and anger have
Become my masters
Which embarrasses me
Exceedingly

Do not know how
Sorrows as mountains
Joys as mustard seeds
Became for me

Chokha says Your praise
My tongue sings not
Great many desires
Burden my head

|| 31 ||

Body is not pure
Caste befouled
Entirely filthy
Vice, virtue

Whatever I try
Is against the mores
What anything else
Should I speak?

Tongue is not pure
Cannot speak proper
Condemned I am
By one and all

To avoid my touch
No one seats near me
Chokha says such is
Life mine

|| 32 ||

Whatever good or bad
Is destined to me
That I will happily
Undergo in life

Now I am not angry
With anyone, O Lord
I have accepted
My own fate

Consequences of past deeds
Make things happen
Why to speak in vain
Of anything else?

Chokha says I am
So embarrassed now
Whatever wrong happened
Was my Karma

|| 33 ||

When I make efforts
Seeking happiness
All of them futile
Seem to me

Sufferings endless
Mind undergoes
Such unrestrained is
My desire

Everything riddled
Appears to me
Better not to speak this
To anyone

Chokha says I am
In such a dilemma
Deliver me at once
Out of this

|| 34 ||

I will speak such language
That You understand
I am not going to hesitate
At all now

What should I do, O Lord
Smothered by persecution
Even You do not reach out
To my rescue

How long should I
Supplicate, O Lord
All my hopes have
Come crashing

Chokha says now
Enough of false hopes
We alone understand
Our own cause

|| 35 ||

Time and again
How much to complain
My source of strength
Has dried up

Not speaking any further
That alone would be wise
Will become a rock
Lying at Your door

Someday, sometime
You might remember me
This only one hope
I hold now

Chokha says then
You will come searching
Till then my mind
I will harden

|| 36 ||

I am but sold
On Your feet
Offering to You all
Faith and life

I have done all
That could be done
You ought to decide
About me

Nine months mother
Carries babe in the womb
The very same is this bond
Between You and me

If own child begging
Goes from lands to lands
Who should be ashamed of?
Chokha asks

|| 37 ||

One's own
One ought to look after
Aren't You aware
Of all of this?

In vain Your boast
Of Your reputation
How many times
Should I say this?

Tolerated this
Till sufferings overwhelmed
Only if eaten is digested
It's of use

Chokha says Yours
I have to tell You
Does all this make me
Look small?

|| 38 ||

I don't understand why
Your heart has hardened
I don't know which
Of my past deeds

How much should I
Recollect my past
That it is affecting
My future

Now it is difficult
Seems unattainable
My mind's mind too
Is engulfed in worries

Chokha says I don't know
What to do
How to assuage
My desire

|| 39 ||

I get no assurance
Nor any reply
Why have you become
So callous

I call You out
With all my passion
What does make You
So frightened?

Say few words to me
That will satisfy me
That is all benefaction
I ask from You

Chokha says fulfil
This wish of mine
Make me not despair
O my Mother

|| 40 ||

Now whimpering
No more in vain
What was to happen
Has happened already

Wherever I be
Dependent I am
And You mercy
Show none

Fate takes its course
Why to despair
We will live happily
With our hopes

Chokha says, to me
This seems to be better
No trouble at all
To my mind

|| 41 ||

I need not salvation
Or the stay in Heaven
Happily in Pandhari
I will live

Whatever hardships
I may have to bear
But leaving Pandhari
I will go nowhere

Even if I don't get
Food to eat here
I will readily survive
On water

Let people abhor
Let them call me fool
That would not hamper
My worship

Chokha says this is
All the bliss I seek
Sorrows and miseries
Anyplace else

|| 42 ||

How do I praise
How do I praise
How do I meditate
Pandurang?

Which way do I
Worship my Lord?
Never is my mind
At peace at all

Restraining this mind
Does not come to hand
How much do I
Worry over it?

Chokha says here
All efforts are futile
How would I find
His feet?

॥ 43 ॥

All alone, seated with me
Speaks of joys and sorrows
Holding my chin
Pacifies me

Pray, do not be
Offended by life
I will tell you
The essence

Whatever that happens
Or that does not
And joys and sorrows
Consequence of Karma

The Lord says, o Chokha
Do not be offended
Swear this to me, my dearest
On my name

|| 44 ||

Why do you consider
Sorrows to be mountains?
I will fulfil wishes
All of yours

The bliss at My door
That is a trove of bliss
Which Namdev already
Has received

That same bliss I will
Bestow upon you
I will bless you
With my grace

You are My life
Dearest of My heart
I will not ever at all
Desert you

Chokha says, O Lord
Indulge my yearning
Hold me close
O Gracious Lord

|| 45 ||

Why should I raise
Mountains of meditation
Or any of the other
Endless rituals?

Why should I go
Far into the wilderness?
Rather in Pandhari
Be a beast

Why should I observe
Fasting and breaking it?
Rather seek company of saints
All the life

Why should I bother
About mores and taboos?
Blissful is companionship
Yours and mine

Why should I roam
Holy places far off?
Rather savour stay
With saints

Why should I indulge
In fire-offering rituals
Rather eat leftovers
At the door of saints

Chokha says bliss
Thus will come home
Surrendering at the feet
Of saints, O Lord

|| 46 ||

Companion You are mine for eternity
Why have you put me in such doubts
I do not find joy or solace anywhere
Except only in Pandhari

Vithoba, do You not know this?
You are the Soul of the world
The Origin and the Supreme Being
Still You ignore the wretched

Pray, there is no justice at Your place
One undergoes sorrows, one rules kingdoms
This is not good conduct at all
It does not become Your reputation

Chokha says how puzzling this is
We understand none of Your deeds
Neither Your grace nor Your wrath
We comprehend, O Vithoba

॥ 47 ॥

My mind has
Resolved this
Nothing else
I would know

Singing the praise
Of the Lord oft
No need to fear
Anyone then

I adore deeply
The Lord's feet
Now none else
Comes to mind

Chokha says the saints
Have made me firm
Hence my mind
Is at peace

॥ 48 ॥

Seeing a Varkari
On way to Pandhari
I will place my forehead
On their feet

With joy, I will
Meet them fondly
Goodness of their hearts
I will rejoice

My parents those
My kith and kin too
I will devote to them
My very existence

Chokha says they are
Source of the Gain Supreme
My saviours of yore
For eternity

|| 49 ||

My anguish, fatigue
Vanished entirely
Seeing Vithoba
On the brick

My life has become
Meaningful now
Having seen His feet
To heart's content

On Chandrabhaga[1] banks
Varkaris dance
Singing the Lord's praise
With a great joy

Flags and emblems
Flock endlessly
Amidst the acclamations
Of the Lord's name

Such joyous celebrations
Rare even for gods
We get effortlessly
Chokha says

1 At Pandharpur, River Bhima takes the shape of a crescent moon, hence the name *Chandrabhaga*, i.e. the Crescent-shaped.

|| 50 ||

O my mind, make
This one resolution
Do not indulge in
Anything else

Those Varkaris
Who go to Pandhari
Happily become a beast
At their home

In their company
Contemplation happens
Bathing in Chandrabhaga
On Ekadashi[1]

Singing the Lord's praise
In the company of saints
Will be an effortless
Gain for me

Chokha says owing to
The company of saints
I will get to join feasts
Along with the rest[2]

1 The eleventh day of Indian lunar calendar which is considered as the sacred-most by the Varkaris.

2 The poet here is referring to the fact that despite his Sainthood, he was never allowed to mingle with others by the so-called upper castes. It was only in the company of the Varkari Saints, that the Poet got equal treatment.

||| 51 |||

They are my kindred
Benefactors, companions
Whoever constantly
Remember Vithoba

In their company
Benefits great many
I found the treasure
In the form of Pandurang

Of the past and future
Got relieved of worries
My near and dear ones
Having met

In their company
Solace and bliss
Whosoever constantly
Remember Vithoba

Chokha says they relieve
From worldly anxieties
The Lord of Vaikuntha[1]
They make visible

1 Lord Vishnu's celestial abode wherein His devotees are believed to attain Salvation.

|| 52 ||

Shame on that conduct
Shame on that thought
Shame on that life
Shame on having borne

Shame on that learning
Shame on those scriptures
Shame on all rituals
Those carried out

Shame on that knowledge
Futile is this talk
Without imbibing kindness
Forgiveness and peace

Shame on that meditation
Shame on those grown hair
Futile is all this routine
Thus followed

Chokha says shame
On such a man ever borne
Hell infinite for him
In the end

|| 53 ||

In the company of sandalwood
Even thorny trees
And wild shrubs smell sweet
Like sandalwood

In the company of saints
The faithless people
Are turned into saints
Themselves too

Chokha says know this
The essence of spirituality
Otherwise be the beast
Of burden

|| 54 ||

Mind is immersed
In endless Samadhi[1]
Remembrance of body
Having forgotten

Fear of taboos, mores
Does not affect Samadhi
Disappeared vainglory
Of possessions

Carrying out chores
Does not affect Samadhi
Absolute purity of mind
Is the only reason

Chokha says such is
The occasion of Samadhi
Knows the peerless
One in a million

1 The state of being in perfect unison with the Supreme Being and the Creation.

|| 55 ||

Beauty of the eye the vision perceived
The eye popped out for the sake of beauty

Beauty of the eye perceived the eye
Inevitably there got closed the eye

Chokha says how wondrous it is
Having perceived beauty the eye dissolved

|| 56 ||

Beyond body, mind; it came to be
The Formless in a form stood here

Behold the Lord, pray all, behold the Lord
Behold the Lord, pray all, within own body

Uncovered Lord manifested in the world
What was naked that engulfed the Lord

Chokha says naked and uncovered became One
Behold, how effortlessly selfhood dissolved

|| 57 ||

Within own body, beheld Pandhari
Soul immortal standing on the brick

Know Him to be the Lord manifest
Peace is Rukmini, the divine consort

Whatever has form gets destroyed
Soul immortal remains Vitthal

Thus the Lord held in his heart
Chokha Mela is welded to His feet

|| 58 ||

Let Mind be
On the Lord
Who resolution
Makes this?

Sense of body
When forgotten
The Lord too
Got dissolved

Inferior is Being
Worship superior
Thence is born
Discrimination

To begin with, exists
No Chokha Mela
How can exist
Pollution?

|| 59 ||

In the ocean of faith
Loaded cargo vessel
Arrived currency
Of Dvaraka[1]

On all the twelve routes
Carries out trade
In the city of Pandhari
Namdev[2]

Chokha says let us
Prostrate at his feet
Let us behold Namdev
Dearest to the Lord

1 The ancient capital city of the Yadav Empire of which Lord Krishna was one of the princes. According to the Varkari legends, Lord Krishna preferred Pandharpur over Dvaraka and settled therein, immersing the latter in the sea.

2 Sant Namdev spread the teachings of the Varkari Sect all over the Indian subcontinent by traversing its length & breadth, performing kirtan at each stop during his journeys. The Poet is referring to this contribution of his Guru in this poem.

|| 60 ||

You have resolved
So many predicaments
Why should I speak
Contrarily?

Till date I was entrapped
By the mess of sensations
That is what seems to have
Caused embarrassment

I see the path
Opened wide for me
Despite the condemnation
Of the world

Chokha says witnessed
This strange happening
That has truly impinged
On my mind

॥ **61** ॥

Anyone who comes
Under its spell
It wreaks havoc
On them

Enough of its sway
Enough of its sway
All it leaves behind
Are endless desires

It deviates the self
From the path of spirituality
How much to persuade
This urchin

Forbidden places
It stubbornly visits
It does what is untoward
Unrestrained

Chokha says, o mind
Swear by yourself
Find contentment
For an instant

|| 62 ||

Just like an ape
Keeps shaking head
Boasts of glory
In the world

Unaware of own good
Unaware of own good
Closes eyes with force
Holds nose[1]

Beads and postures
Such masquerades
Swinging bodies
But no essence

Hounded by hunger
Creates façade
Goes asking for alms
Door to door

Chokha says such
Fraudsters in the world
Who would call them
Sadhu, O Lord?

1 Here, the reference is to the fake yogis who know nothing beyond physical manoeuvres like asanas and mudras.

|| 63 ||

Elaborate banquet
Sitting to feast on
Houseflies kill
The appetite

Ultimate nature
When debased
What to expect
Otherwise

Nature of the dog
Even when seated on throne
Goes looking for
But excreta

Does not recognize
Own and strangers
Barks incessantly
By nature

Chokha says such
Is the life of the wicked
Ever despicable
In the world

|| 64 ||

In the company of the low-born
The Lord became polluted
By cleansing with water
Made Him pure

To begin with, pure
Is the Lord at all?
It's like making the eye
To see the eye

Within the pure
Resides the Pure
Why doesn't the impure
Reside in the impure?

Chokha says the Lord
Is above the both
To the content of my eyes
Him I beheld

|| 65 ||

Equally polluting are
All Five Elements[1]
That the entire world
Is made of

Then how can one be pure
And the other impure
If the origin of pollution
Is our bodies?

In the beginning and end
Nothing but pollution
Pure can be anyone
Which way?

Chokha says to me
This puzzles a lot
Beyond pollution
Is anyone at all?

1 The five elements of nature: Earth, Air, Fire, Water & Sky. All the human beings, just like the remainder of the Creation, are said to be formed out of these Five Great Elements.

|| 66 ||

Who be the pure?
Who be the impure?
Beyond the both
Vitthal mine

Who got polluted?
By which means?
Conceived essentially
As the Pure

Pollution of the Five[1]
Within one body
Then pure in the world
How can be any?

Chokha says mine
Vitthal alone is pure
Despite being formless
Stands on the brick

1 The Five Great Elements.

|| 67 ||

Polluted by Time
Both the being and the Beyond
Confined to this world
With unyielding bonds

Pollution, pollution
All over the universe
Encompasses living, non-living
Nothing but pollution

Pollution in joys
Pollution in sorrows
Pollution in pollution
Has thrived

The womb of pollution
Bears the fruit of pollution
Chokha the unadulterated
Sings the Lord's praise

ଔଔଔ || 68 || ഋഋഋ

Once such a wonder happened
The Lord unexpectedly arrived

Arriving, sat on the verandah
Said, "Give me something to eat"

Jani1 said, "O dear Lord
Go, have by Your own hands"

The Lord searched everything
Found the earthen pot covered

Rushing forth the Lord went
Returned with broken rice

Holding Jani's hand
Put morsels in her mouth

Both happily had the meal
Belching with contentment

Chokha stood outside
Begging for the leftovers

1 Sant Namdev's maidservant, Jani or Janabai was a Saint-poet of highest caliber, perhaps the first woman to speak against patriarchy in her poems.

|| 69 ||

Here I have company
Only of the wicked
That saddens me
All the time

My own community
Have to eat impious
Liquor and meat
Their meals comprise

Others call me names
Speaking out filth
That hurts my heart
To no end

Chokha says thus
I am to go nowhere
Pray, how long should I
Suffer all this?

|| 70 ||

Such are the ways
Of this world
What should I say
Of its vices, virtues?

Debased is the caste
Nameless existence
How can one be kith
Or kin to anyone?

Sycophants, thieves, womanizers
Corrupt through and through
Debased existence for eternity
Is their destiny

Chokha says I suffer
In the company of such
Separation from you
Anguishes me

|| 71 ||

Here for me nothing
But mountains of sorrows
My mind bewails
All the while

O Lord Resident of Pandhari
Why have you sent me away?
I find none of my own here
What do I do?

I long for Pandhari
I long for Your door
Gatherings of the saints
I long for

I long for Namdev
Pundalik dearest
Chokha says behold
I lie in distress

||72||

Whenever I will be released
This my mind thinks ever
Why am I entrapped
Here, O Lord?

Now please rush
To my rescue
Release me, O Hari
From here

Upon my life
I beseech You
What makes You
Take so long?

Chokha says waste
No time further
I see my end
Pretty nigh

|| 73 ||

My end is nigh
It seems to me
What was destined
Has happened

From birth, dependent
Have been servant Yours
Now in the end
I lie far away

Have lost all hopes
Of Your leftovers
Fate has taken
Its course

Chokha says mine
Prostration at Your feet
Take me in shelter
Of Your grace

॥ 74 ॥

Unrestrained mind
Brings on frenzy
Goes wandering far
Beyond reach

Upon its feet
Put shackles firm
No more troubles
From it then

It will stay ever still
Such is this measure
Know not ways
Any other

Chokha says whatever
You have taught
That has borne fruit
O Namdev

|| 75 ||

Absolute love
Brought the Absolute
The Absolute assumed
The form Absolute

Absolute endearing
Absolute elegant
Absolute dissolves
In the Absolute

Absolute bliss
From the Absolute
Absolute manifestation
Of the Absolute

Chokha says the Absolute
Revealed to Namdev
The Absolute he showed
To me as well

ೞೞೞ || 76 || ೞೞೞ

What to perceive
What to worship
What to sing
For whom

Where to go
Where to stay
Where to look
For what

Where be joy
Where be sorrow
Where to seek
All of which

Chokha says
Namdev judicious
Sensed the conundrum
Conveyed to me

|| 77 ||

Golden is this day
Of great fortune
I met in person
Namdev

Mine he gave me
Mine he gave me
Mine he gave me
Bliss of love

Much longing
After great efforts
My mind brims with
Bliss of bliss

The Lord mine he showed
Within my own being
Dissolved then and there
Sense of selfhood

Chokha says solace
Of my mind he is
Hence I sing praise
Of Namdev

|| 78 ||

So debased caste
Body too impure
Not knowing pure
Unadulterated

Still, he bestowed
His grace upon me
Destroyed ignorance
Muddled up

Great condemnation
From great many
All of it ineffective
By his grace

Therefore, my mind
Welded to his feet
Chokha says further
What to speak

|| 79 ||

What marketplace? Whose sack?
Distinct always is the Owner

Goods belong to whom? Who is the seller?
All the transactions remain undisclosed

On the sun setting, closes the marketplace
All hustle and bustle go away

Chokha says the measure is brimming to top
In whose hands should I empty it?

|| 80 ||

Whose companionship
To seek? For whom?
Nothing but sorrows
Engulfing thence

Hence Namdev's
Feet I have held
On remembering them
Contentment

Bliss of bliss
He showed me
Joy incarnate
On the brick

Chokha says life
Namdev is mine
Prostrate I lie
In front of him

☙☙☙ || 81 || ❧❧❧

Bliss unparalleled
At the feet of the saint
In person at Alandi
He resides

He is my lord
Dnyaneshwar Mauli1
Who uncovered the essence
Of the Upanishadas2

For the sake of
The upliftment
Of all the downtrodden
And the desire-bound

Chokha says glorious
The treatise, Dnyandevi
On reading it, the beings
Find the Lord

1 *Mauli* (माउली) means mother. This is the title that the Varkari tradition has lovingly bestowed upon Sant Dnyandev, aka Dnyaneshwar, for his contribution in giving the contemporary society a new direction.

2 Here, the Poet refers to Dnyandev's seminal work, Dnyaneshwari or Dnyandevi, a groundbreaking commentary upon Bhagvad Gita. Dnyaneshwari provides the ethical/philosophical foundation to the Varkari Sect.

|| 82 ||

You are my Mother
You are my Mother
You are my Mother
O Vitthal

Why did you forsake me?
Why separated me from You?
Why did You send me
To Mangalvedha[1]?

Had I become such
A burden for You
That You distanced me
From Your feet?

Chokha says I do not
Care for the wages
When I can sing sweet
Praise of Yours

1 A town not far from Pandarpur where the Poet was taken to work on the construction of town-wall. Unfortunately, the wall collapsed killing many of the labourers, including the Poet. This poem and the next were composed during his stay at Mangalvedha.

|| 83 ||

All that I desire
Is to behold Your feet
There is nothing else
I long for

Bestow upon me
Your grace ever
And blissful stay
Next to Namdev's

Give me place
At Your door
This is all, O Lord
I ask of You

Chokha says today
I feel dejected
Moment to moment
Longing for Pandhari

|| 84 ||

Mine own have become
Strangers for me
It amazes me
Amusingly

I toiled day and night
For all of them
Mine own have turned
Their backs on me

Good-bad, my own morsels
I fed in their mouths
I nourished their beings
For their happiness

Chokha says I became
All alone, all alone
All ran away
Seeing hardships

|| 85 ||

Abandoning those in Your refuge
What are you going to gain?
Scriptures narrate ancient tales
All of them in vain

Rejecting those in Your refuge
That will be such a shame
I will proclaim this to all
Know this my resolve

Why is that motto[1] tied at Your feet?
Just throw, throw it away, O Lord
Tall tales of Your benevolence
No one to rescue me

Chokha says You are omniscient
Vedas know not Your pre-eminence
Upanishads too admit ignorance
What me wretched is to say

1 Lord Vitthal wears anklets which have inscriptions, declaring the Lord to be the Protector of His worshippers.

|| 86 ||

You brought me up
You nurtured me
You alone showed
This world to me

Your ways and means
You alone know
We very well know
Our own cause

What is it, O Lord
That makes You hesitate?
Pray, tell me, O Lord
But only this

Chokha says what more
Should I speak?
You are my Saviour
O Lord of the lords

|| 87 ||

Just once rid me, O Lord
Of this burning anguish
Then I will not ever
Grumble again

Remembering Your feet
Will remain satisfied
That bliss in heart
I will cherish

Attachments and desires
I have relinquished
I bank upon You
Every which way

Chokha says now
Relieve me from this maze
This riddle of life
Frightening, O Lord

|| 88 ||

Now no more at all
Fascination for these
Disgust I am filled with
For the worldly matters

Food gone bad
How repulses one
Same happens to me
Regarding this

Now all of these
Sources of miseries
I cannot bear
Patiently anymore

Chokha says enough
Of these worldly matters
They take me away
From the Supreme Gain

|| 89 ||

Pollution for Vedas
Pollution for Shastras
Puranas[1] are filled with
Demeaning pollution

Pollution for the being
Pollution for the Beyond
Body is filled with
Demeaning pollution

Pollution for Brahma
Pollution for Vishnu
Pollution for Shankar
Demeaning

Pollution in the birth
Pollution in the death
Chokha says pollution
Origin to End

1 Ancient Indian religious texts that consist mainly of mythology.

|| 90 ||

I have made this
Resolve in my mind
Your tempting, O Lord
Enough now

My burdens on You
Heaped I have all
This I know myself
Well indeed

Speaking trifles
Seems worthless
I do not have much
Strength in me

Chokha says happily
I will sit protesting
That will only dent
Your eminence

|| 91 ||

Not bothering whether
It seems good or bad
I will proclaim the truth
Far and wide, O Lord

Now how long
Should I hesitate?
You apparently
Know it well

"The Protector" motto
Flaunts on Your anklet
Reputed in Three Worlds
You are such

Chokha says whatever
That harms not Your glory
Undertake such a course
Better, O Lord

|| 92 ||

Ceremonial thread adorning waist
That is the goldsmith Narhari[1]

Tinklets on feet chime sweetly
That is the dearest Namdev

Anklet on the left foot
Sounds prominently Parisa[2]

Anklet on the right foot
Sings aloud the songs of Jaidev[3]

The beautiful feet on the brick
That is, know well, Chokha Mela

1 A Varkari Saint, the Poet's contemporary
2 A Varkari Saint, the Poet's contemporary
3 A 12th century devotional poet, well-known for his Geet Govinda

|| 93 ||

Love infinite
Namdev obtained
That we received
For eternity

Therefore, in Pandhari
On the banks of Bhima
Where the Lord on the brick
Hands on hips

Sins extraordinaire
Are absolved at sight
Such is the boon
Granted to Pundalik

For twenty-eight eons
Has not sat down
With joined feet
Still standing

Chokha says such is
The Protector of devotees
Compassionate towards
The faithful

|| 94 ||

Somewhere one
Somewhere two
But in Pandhari
The Absolute

Somewhere deity
Somewhere holy water
But in Pandhari
Everything

Somewhere thrones
Somewhere robes
But in Pandhari
Feet on the brick

Somewhere sleeping
Somewhere sitting
But in Pandhari
Always standing

Chokha says
Whatever wherever
But in Pandhari
With open arms

|| 95 ||

The Lord is standing
The Lord is standing
The Lord is standing
On the brick

Within all beings
The Lord is standing
Beauty of the Cosmos
In Pandhari

Pray, behold the Lord
Pray, behold the Lord
Standing with joined feet
On the brick

Chokha says ours
Blissful trove of bliss
Our patrimony
In Pandhari

|| 96 ||

Sufferings of eternity
Who else will rid of?
Persecuted in this world
Rescue me, O Lord

I surrender at Your feet
O Lord of the Yadavas
Allaying all my fears
Help me cross this ocean

Without You who will
Take me out of this maze?
I have become insane
I see no solution

Chokha says, O Lord Almighty
Now allay this anguish of life
I rest my head, O Vitthal
On Your feet

|| 97 ||

Showing mercy
Protect me, O Lord

I am wretched, wretched
Surrendered at Your feet

Such a shame it will be for You
On abandoning me, O Lord

Preserve Your reputation
Promising me shelter

Chokha says, O Lord
Now hesitate not at all

॥ 98 ॥

Anxious my mind
Rambles helter-skelter
Rescue me from this
O Lord of the lords

I have become restless
What should I do now?
Not able to restrain
The unrestrained

This racket is Yours
You better get rid of it
Please take us out
Of all this

Chokha says then alone
My mind will find bliss
Enough of the sorrows
Henceforth, O Lord

|| 99 ||

How my mind
Longs for it!
Does not wish for
Anything else

En route to Pandhari
Arrive Varkaris
Talking to them
Is such a bliss

Those who sing
Praise of my Vitthal
My source of bliss
Those Varkaris

Having arrived, I will
Prostrate in front of them
Happily, I will take them
In my arms

Chokha says they are
Life of my life
I will receive them
With utmost devotion

|| 100 ||

Salutation, o my parents, salutation[1]
I am Mahar of Your Mahar

Have got exceedingly hungry
Have come for Your leftovers[2]

Have come with great hopes
I am servant of Your servant

Chokha says this basket
Have brought for Your leftovers

1 Being placed at the bottom of the caste hierarchy, it was mandatory for all the 'outcastes' to greet the so-called upper caste people with reverence by bending as low as possible, head almost touching the ground.

2 The members of the Mahar community had to beg for their livelihood, despite performing all their laborious duties. At the end of the day, they would go from door to door shouting salutations (*johaar* in Marathi) for the master and the lady of the house, carrying a bamboo basket to collect the stale food that would be dropped from a distance in that basket.

APPENDIX

A distinct feature of all major Varkari Saint-poets is that a large number of 'satellite poets' also composed poems under their influence. Chokha Mela also has his satellite poets in his family members - Soyara, his wife; Nirmala, his sister; Karma Mela, his son; and Banka, Nirmala's husband. Each of these are great poets on their own and also provide important biographical details about Chokha Mela. What caliber these four have, one can get a fair idea from these specimen poems.

SOYARA

All colours One became
In colours is coloured the Colour Supreme

Selfhood has gone to waste
On seeing the Lord of Pandhari

No place for discrimination
Ran away the anger, the lust

Despite being, you are Beyond
Ever in Samadhi, behold

Beholder, beholding have vanished
Says Chokha's Mahari[1]

***

1 This is how Soyara addresses herself in her poems, a unique signature style indeed! She is perhaps the first person to appropriate a term that was supposed to be an insult (a very postmodern phenomenon) and goes on, instead, to flaunt it proudly in all her poems!

NIRMALA

All this while
You protected him
Forgiving Chokha
All his offences

After he is gone
Are You tired of us?
Please tell me this
O Lord

Debased, wretched me
Committed endless sins
I surrender at Your feet
With all my being

Nirmala says, O Lord
You are compassionate
Hence protect me
As Your own

***

BANKA

The lord of the learned
Dnyaneshwar Mauli
Showered his grace
On Khechar[1]

On Dnyandev's feet
Surrendered Khechar
Who graced Namdev
Absolutely

Namdev placed his hand
On Chokha's head
Blessed him by teaching
Three syllables, Vitthala

Banka says mine
Chokha is Guru
I lie prostrate
At his feet
***

Chokha pure, unadulterated
No stain at all in his being

Chokha is the ocean of bliss
Chokha is the field of devotion

Chokha is mother affectionate
Chokha is the shelter of grace

Chokha is the solace of my mind
Banka lies prostrate in front of him
***

1 Visoba Khechar was a Brahmin of Alandi village who incessantly persecuted Dnyandev and his siblings initially, only to become one of their most ardent followers. He happens to be Sant Namdev's Guru.

KARMA MELA

You created our caste the basest
Why don't You understand, O Lord?

Whole life spent eating leftovers
You don't feel ashamed of it

At our home, curd and rice
You ate, how can you deny?

Says Chokha's Karma Mela
Why did You give me birth?
***

Our father's savings
Why don't You return it to us?

How is this conduct of Yours?
Pleading, I have exhausted, O Lord

How many times to and fro
Meaninglessly, should I go?

Karma Mela says, O Lord
How long should I plead thus?
***

Sitaram Mhatre Foundation's Other Publication

THE AUTOBIOGRAPHY OF SANT BAHINABAI

Sant Bahinabai (1628-1700) was just three years old when she was married off to a 30-year-old widower. Here starts a long series of hardships that Bahinabai had to brave out for the better part of her life. Hardly had she turned seven, when she had to leave their native place along with her family and go in search of livelihood from village to village and town to town, and that too on foot. No one knew when or where the next meal would be. To worsen the matters, Bahinabai's short tempered husband accompanied her family during these seemingly endless journeys and Bahinabai was subjected to the most brutal form of domestic violence at the hands of her husband from a very tender age (even when she was three months pregnant). This travesty of a married life continued for almost a decade and her birth in the so-called higher caste did next to nothing to alleviate Bahinabai's misery, just like millions of women before and after her. What makes Bahinabai's sufferings significant is the fact that she gave them a voice in her poems and became the first woman autobiographer of India. Her autobiography ranks very high among those works that document the lives of survivors of domestic violence, apart from being one of the oldest, if not THE oldest, such an account in the history of world literature. With its uninhibited attacks on patriarchy, Bahinabai's autobiography predates all the feminist texts in the world. This book also contains Bahinabai's translation of Vajrasuchi Upanishad, which makes her the first woman translator of India.

9 788196 091125

Printed at Repro India Ltd.